A SEASON OF POSSIBILITIES

HOWARD BOOKS
A DIVISION OF SIMON & SCHUSTER
New York   London   Toronto   Sydney

MAL AUSTIN

picture · psalms   *an illustrated meditation*

INTRODUCTION

Why does it seem we feel closer to God when we are immersed in a natural or idyllic or wild setting? And then even more so at dawn or dusk?

We know by scripture and experience that a loving God who never sleeps and is not influenced by the concept of time is accessible to us at any time and any place. Yet we also know that our life, our world, is one of seasons. Our days, our bodies, our emotions, and even the ease with which we find God are ever changing in nature and intensity according to weather, seasons, sunlight, time, and so on.

Many years ago, I experienced a powerful unplanned early-morning rising, as if being pulled out of bed by a magnet. I was saturated as I walked in the long wet grass around my lily pond, camera working furiously, seeing common old reeds in new ways; my mind raced with words of poetry to be remembered and written later as the sun rose. This was a deeply impacting mystical experience that left me with new words of praise and worship for the Creator. As a landscape photographer I have had many similar experiences since.

I've often wondered if the explanation for such encounters could be this simple—perhaps we were designed to meet God in a garden. The garden in Genesis was made especially for Adam by God—some garden it was! Every type of plant as well as every need for the new humans was supplied there. As my art demands that I spend much time in this world's present gardens, both ordered and wild, I have discovered that the human life experience is all there, laid out before us!

A life-size model of life itself is all around: cycles, seasons, strength, love, fruit, provision, abundance, color, fragrance, texture, reproduction, health, order, structure, timing, change, growth, movement, size, variety, and community. But the now fallen garden also displays death, decay, weakness, enmity, disease, pests, scarcity, competition, weeds, thorns, and the absence of permanence or eternity.

There are two unique additions with our presence—soul and spirit. It's these extra dimensions, fully intended, wonderfully designed, that allow us greater purpose in this garden—connection and communication, just a little of what was begun with Adam and Eve.

As such, we love walking through the garden. It is designed as a gift to us; we were not designed to just be another ingredient. It is a world, it is a mirror! All of us have viewed gardens from a similar distance as we walk through them or work in them; few of us take the time to bend down and examine them close up, and so we miss so much. Psalm 139 talks about a God who doesn't just walk by us but looks at us very closely and knows us well. That is why these images are mostly close up.

His garden is so varied, so colorful, so straight, so curved, so shaped, and so different all over the world, just like His children.

About the Photographer

MAL AUSTIN is one of Australia's most prominent Christian artists with a camera. A former schoolteacher, Mal now devotes his time to capturing the beauty of nature and crafting it into posters, gift cards, calendars, and books.

Eighteen years of commercial photography saw him complete over 650 weddings and hundreds of family portraits and advertising assignments. In 2000, Mal began a new photographic direction and vision under the name of Givenworks, believing God had given him new works to do. He specializes in the use of a panoramic film camera, and his work takes him deep into the Australian and New Zealand countryside to capture many isolated places with untouched landscapes.

Mal also works in close-up floral images with an emphasis on color, pattern, shape, and texture. While some images used in this book are from large-format Pentax and Bronica film cameras, most are digitally captured using Nikon D70 and D80 cameras.

www.givenworks.com

COLOR:
What a gift color is! God has blessed us with billions of colors for our use and pleasure—each as unique and special as we are. God recognizes the value of different.

LIGHT:
Any subject suddenly comes alive when a sliver of morning light hits it. Jesus is our morning light, bringing us to life, and changing us for the better.

CLOSE-UP:
God is a God of details. Look closely and you will see beauty in every feature. Don't be afraid to draw close to God. Beauty increases in closeness.

SHAPE:
Every leaf and every petal is unique by design and is then changed by weather and time. But our changes are best coming from God's Spirit.

TEXTURE:
Smooth, rough, sharp, scaly; textures create interest in nature. Let time, choices, and life's experience work to form beautiful patterns in us as well.

ENVIRONMENT:
God's environment places dew, light, sun, food, and life cycles necessary for each plant to grow. He not only meets our needs but shapes our lives in extra dimensions.

BUGS:
Even though it's often hard to see, the beauty, color, and shapes of the tiny world of bugs is around us all. God uses even the smallest of creatures for His purpose.

AGING:
Plants have a life cycle, just as we do. Each stage brings beautiful new shapes and rich, powerful colors. God loves and values life in all its glorious stages.

IN SITU:
All the images in this book were taken in their natural place of growth. We, too, grow best in the place God has chosen for us.

PSALM 91

A God Who Protects

I trust you

THOSE WHO GO TO GOD MOST HIGH FOR SAFETY
WILL BE PROTECTED BY THE ALMIGHTY.
I WILL SAY TO THE LORD,
"YOU ARE MY PLACE OF SAFETY AND PROTECTION.
YOU ARE MY GOD AND I TRUST YOU."

God will save you

GOD WILL SAVE
YOU FROM
HIDDEN TRAPS
AND FROM
DEADLY DISEASES.
HE WILL COVER
YOU WITH HIS
FEATHERS,
AND UNDER
HIS WINGS
YOU CAN HIDE.
HIS TRUTH WILL BE
YOUR SHIELD
AND PROTECTION.

You will not fear any danger by night
or an arrow during the day.
You will not be afraid of diseases
that come in the dark
or sickness that strikes at noon.

AT YOUR SIDE ONE
THOUSAND PEOPLE MAY DIE,
OR EVEN TEN THOUSAND
RIGHT BESIDE YOU,
BUT YOU WILL NOT BE HURT.
YOU WILL ONLY WATCH AND
SEE THE WICKED PUNISHED.

Fear Not

a place of safety

The Lord is your protection;
you have made God Most High
your place of safety.
Nothing bad will happen to you;
no disaster will come to your home.

HE HAS PUT HIS ANGELS
IN CHARGE OF YOU
TO WATCH OVER YOU
WHEREVER YOU GO.
THEY WILL
CATCH YOU
IN THEIR HANDS
SO THAT YOU WILL NOT
HIT YOUR FOOT
ON A ROCK.

they watch over you

They will call to me,
and I will answer them.
I will be with them
in trouble;
I will rescue them
and honor them.

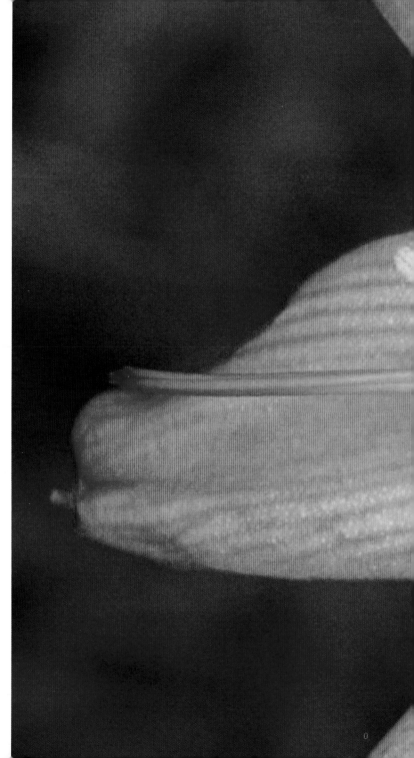

I will save

THE LORD SAYS,
"WHOEVER LOVES
ME, I WILL SAVE.
I WILL PROTECT
THOSE WHO
KNOW ME.
I WILL GIVE THEM
A LONG, FULL LIFE,
AND THEY WILL
SEE HOW
I CAN SAVE."

PSALM 84

A God Who Welcomes

your dwelling place

How lovely is your
dwelling place,
O LORD
Almighty!
My soul yearns,
even faints,
for the courts of the
LORD;
my heart and
my flesh cry out
for the living God.

my King and my God

EVEN THE SPARROW
HAS FOUND A HOME,
AND THE SWALLOW
A NEST FOR HERSELF,
WHERE SHE MAY HAVE HER YOUNG —
A PLACE NEAR YOUR ALTAR,
O LORD ALMIGHTY,
MY KING AND MY GOD.

Blessed are those
who dwell in your house;
they are ever praising you. . . .

Blessed are those
whose strength is in you,
who have set their hearts
on pilgrimage.

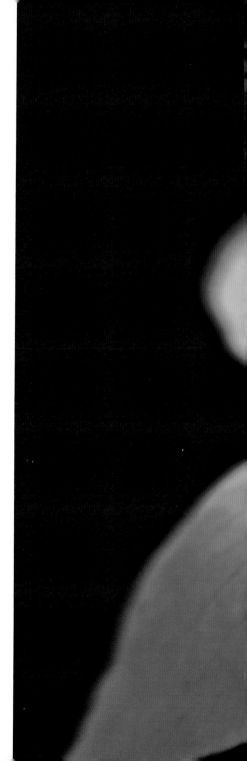

ever praising You

As they pass through
the Valley of Baca,
they make it a place of springs;
the autumn rains
also cover it with pools.
They go from strength to strength,
till each appears before God in Zion.

God's Strength

one day in your courts

BETTER IS ONE DAY IN YOUR COURTS
THAN A THOUSAND ELSEWHERE;
I WOULD RATHER BE A DOORKEEPER
IN THE HOUSE OF MY GOD
THAN DWELL IN THE TENTS OF THE WICKED.

For the LORD God is a sun and shield;
the LORD bestows favor and honor;
no good thing does he withhold
from those whose walk is blameless.
O LORD Almighty,
blessed is the man who trusts in you.

PSALM 111

A God Who Frees

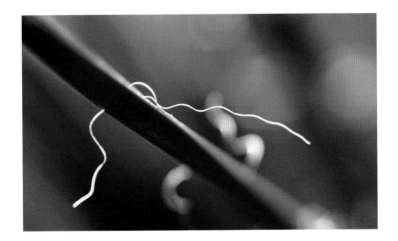

THE LORD DOES GREAT THINGS;
THOSE WHO ENJOY THEM SEEK THEM.
WHAT HE DOES IS GLORIOUS AND SPLENDID,
AND HIS GOODNESS CONTINUES FOREVER.

True and right

He has shown
his people his power
when he gave them the lands
of other nations.
Everything he does
is good and fair;
all his orders can be trusted.
They will continue forever.
They were made
true and right.

Unforgettable

His
miracles
are unforgettable.
The Lord
is kind
and merciful.
He gives
food to those
who fear him.
He remembers
his agreement
forever.

Everlasting

HE SETS
HIS PEOPLE FREE.
HE MADE
HIS AGREEMENT
EVERLASTING.
HE IS HOLY
AND WONDERFUL.

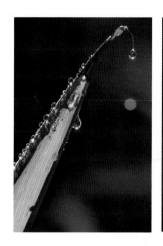

Wisdom begins with
respect for the Lord;
those who obey
his orders have
good understanding.
He should be
praised forever.

Understanding

Our purpose at Howard Books is to:
• *Increase faith* in the hearts of growing Christians
• *Inspire holiness* in the lives of believers
• *Instill hope* in the hearts of struggling people everywhere
Because He's coming again!

Published by Howard Books, a Division of Simon & Schuster, Inc.
1230 Avenue of the Americas, New York, NY 10020
www.howardpublishing.com

Picture Psalms: A Season of Possibilities © 2007 by Mal Austin

ISBN-13: 978-1-4165-5037-2
ISBN-10:   1-4165-5037-2
10 9 8 7 6 5 4 3 2 1

First Howard hardcover edition January 2008

Manufactured in China

For information regarding special discounts for bulk purchases, please contact Simon & Schuster Special Sales at 1-800-456-6798 or business@simonandschuster.com.

Edited by Chrys Howard
Cover and interior design by Stephanie D. Walker